M

ATT
and

WHEN: 1690s

WHEREs: Coast of India

MAP GRID REFERENCE: I, 4

CAPE CASTLE

SLAVE SHIPS ATTACKED BY:
Black Bart and other pirates

WHEN: 1719

WHERE: Atlantic Ocean

MAP GRID REFERENCE: F, 4

TRIREME REPLICA

ATTACKED BY: Polycrates

WHEN: 520s and 530s BCE

WHERE: Aegean Sea and coast of Asia Minor

MAP GRID REFERENCE: G, 3

Silver Dolphin Books
An imprint of Printers Row Publishing Group
10350 Barnes Canyon Road, Suite 100,
San Diego, CA 92121
www.silverdolphinbooks.com

Written by: Philip Steele
Paper Engineer: Alan Young
Illustrators: Laszlo Veres, Nick Harris, Adam Hook, Richard Hook, Peter Bull,
Francis Philips, Mike Saunders, Martin Saunders, Arpad Olbey/Beehive Illustration

Designed and Edited by Tall Tree Ltd
Editor: Emma Marriott
Designer: Jonathan Vipond

Printers Row Publishing Group is a division of Readerlink Distribution Services, LLC.
Silver Dolphin Books is a registered trademark of Readerlink Distribution Services, LLC.

All notations of errors or omissions should be addressed to Silver Dolphin Books, Editorial
Department, at the above address. All other correspondence (author inquiries, permissions)
concerning the content of this book should be addressed to Quarto Children's Books Ltd,
The Old Brewery, 6 Blundell Street,
London N7 9BH UK.

ISBN: 978-1-62686-950-9

Manufactured, printed, and assembled in Shaoguan, China.
First printing, July 2017. SL/07/17.

21 20 19 18 17 1 2 3 4 5

TREASURE HUNTERS

WRITTEN BY

PHILIP STEELE

CONTENTS

Danger on the High Seas

Ships at sea are sometimes at the mercy of nature. But even a raging storm can be less terrifying than an attack by pirates. Whether it was poverty or a thirst for adventure that drove the pirates to attack, they all had one thing in common. They were treasure hunters—searching the seas for precious gold and gems.

GREED AND GUNPOWDER

Pirates have sailed the oceans almost as long as boats have existed. This book tells a story of greed and gunpowder, of hurricanes and treachery, of fighting and fury, set amid tropical islands and cold northern seas.

NAMES FOR A PIRATE

The word "pirate" comes from a word in the Ancient Greek language, meaning a "chancer" or a surprise attacker. Pirates throughout history have been called sea people, sea robbers, corsairs, rovers, buccaneers, sea dogs, Vikings, freebooters, or filibusters.

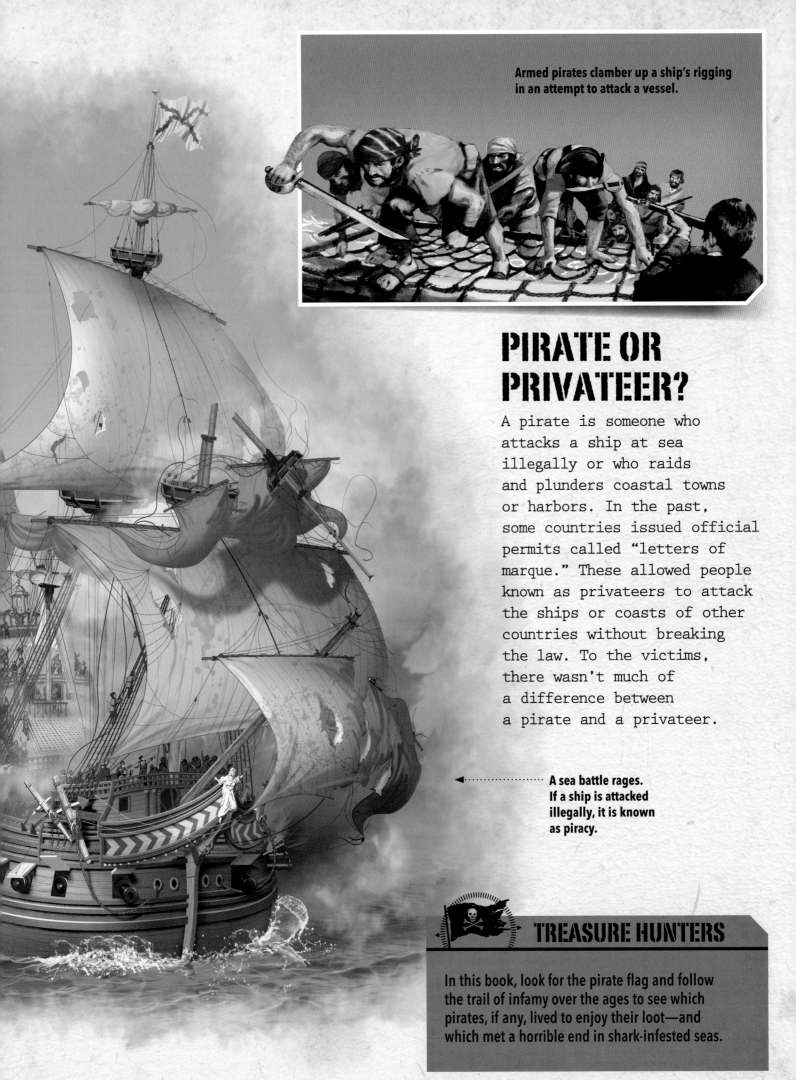

Armed pirates clamber up a ship's rigging in an attempt to attack a vessel.

PIRATE OR PRIVATEER?

A pirate is someone who attacks a ship at sea illegally or who raids and plunders coastal towns or harbors. In the past, some countries issued official permits called "letters of marque." These allowed people known as privateers to attack the ships or coasts of other countries without breaking the law. To the victims, there wasn't much of a difference between a pirate and a privateer.

◄········· A sea battle rages. If a ship is attacked illegally, it is known as piracy.

TREASURE HUNTERS

In this book, look for the pirate flag and follow the trail of infamy over the ages to see which pirates, if any, lived to enjoy their loot—and which met a horrible end in shark-infested seas.

A Timeline of Piracy

From tropical islands to stormy northern seas, pirates have spread fear and created mayhem for almost as long as ships have sailed the seas. The history of piracy is one of desperate battles at sea, of cruelty, treachery, and revenge . . . all for the glint of gold and a chest full of treasure.

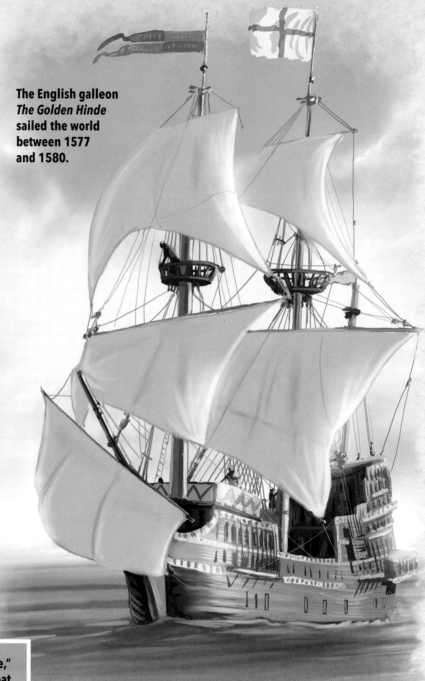

The English galleon *The Golden Hinde* sailed the world between 1577 and 1580.

Early Piracy
500 BCE–1492

Around 500 BCE, piracy was a way of life in the Greek islands. The Roman general Pompey fought against Mediterranean pirates in 67 BCE. Viking pirates terrorized Europe around 790 CE.

Picture of a "trireme," an ancient Greek boat with three rows of oars.

The Wider World
1492–1630

This was the great age of European exploration. From 1566 onward, the Spanish sent convoys of galleons (large ships with three or more decks) from the Americas back to Spain, packed with treasure. They risked being attacked by pirates or wrecked by hurricanes.

Pirate Captain Keitt, who was active in the Caribbean in the 1600s.

THE PIRATE ROUND 1690—1720

Pirate captains sailed from the Americas to Africa and the Indian Ocean, looting all the way and back again. This route was known as the Pirate Round.

Pirates bury their stolen treasure chest.

THE BUCCANEERS 1630—1690

The Caribbean islands and the northern coastline of South America controlled by Spain, known as the "Spanish Main," was a center of piracy until the 1700s. Here, rebels, adventurers, and cruel men attacked treasure-laden ships passing near their shores.

A soldier aims his gun at a Somalian pirate ship.

WAR ON PIRACY 1720—PRESENT

The 1800s saw major sea battles, with the aim to end piracy. Since the 1990s, piracy has increased again in the Indian Ocean. And war ships have been sent to protect international shipping.

ANCIENT PIRACY

More than 3,000 years ago, cargo ships sailed the trading routes around the eastern Mediterranean Sea and the Red Sea. They were laden with gold, rubies, copper, cedarwood, dyes, rich textiles, and gold. The Phoenicians, who lived in the coastal areas of the eastern Mediterranean, were the greatest seafarers and traders of the region.

VIOLENT SEAFARING

But not all parts of the Mediterranean were prosperous. There were many rocky, barren coasts with inlets and coves where ships could hide away. For many centuries, seafarers from the region of Cilicia (now in southern Turkey), the Greek islands, and the shores of Illyria (modern Albania) experienced cruel and violent attacks.

A PROBLEM FOR THE PHARAOHS

There are many references in Egyptian art to raids on shipping at sea and on coasts. The "sea people" who terrorized the Mediterranean Sea between 1276 and 1178 BCE may have been pirates.

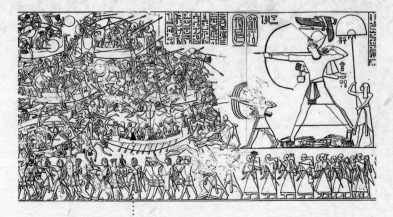

An ancient wall relief shows Egyptians attacking the "sea people."

A Roman merchant ship with large steering oars.

ENEMIES OF ROME

In the days of Ancient Rome, it was reported that pirate fleets of up to 1,000 prowled the Mediterranean Sea. The numbers may have been exaggerated, and the Romans tended to refer to all their enemies at sea as "pirates." In 75 BCE, when Julius Caesar was 25 years old, he was captured by Silician pirates. They demanded a ransom for his freedom, which was paid. Julius Caesar then sailed back to capture the pirates and had them crucified.

Julius Caesar was kidnapped by pirates who demanded a hefty ransom for his return.

A Phoenician merchant ship unloads goods, such as wood and wine.

☠ TREASURE HUNTERS

Polycrates (538–522 BCE)

The Greek island of Samos had a reputation for piracy. The island's ruler from about 538 to 522 BCE was named Polycrates. He was a powerful and successful ruler, who built a large fleet of warships. He was feared as someone who attacked and robbed the ships of his friends as well as his enemies and who plundered the islands of the Aegean Sea and the coasts of Asia Minor (modern Turkey).

Ancient Greek Tales
Over 2,700 years ago, the Greek poet Homer wrote the *Odyssey*, an exciting tale of adventures and sea voyages. In the story, Homer depicts piracy as harmful to trade, but also adventurous and brave and as a fair way to win wealth and fame.

A warship scene from the Greek tale, the *Odyssey*.

THE DRAGON SHIPS

Around 1,200 years ago, many people along the coasts and rivers of Europe lived in fear. When ships with prows shaped into mythical beasts appeared on the horizon, villagers hid their silver and reached for their swords. Soon, armed pirates were leaping ashore. The attackers were known as Northmen or Danes and later became known as Vikings. They came from the modern-day lands of Norway, Sweden, and Denmark. Seafaring and raiding were part of their everyday life.

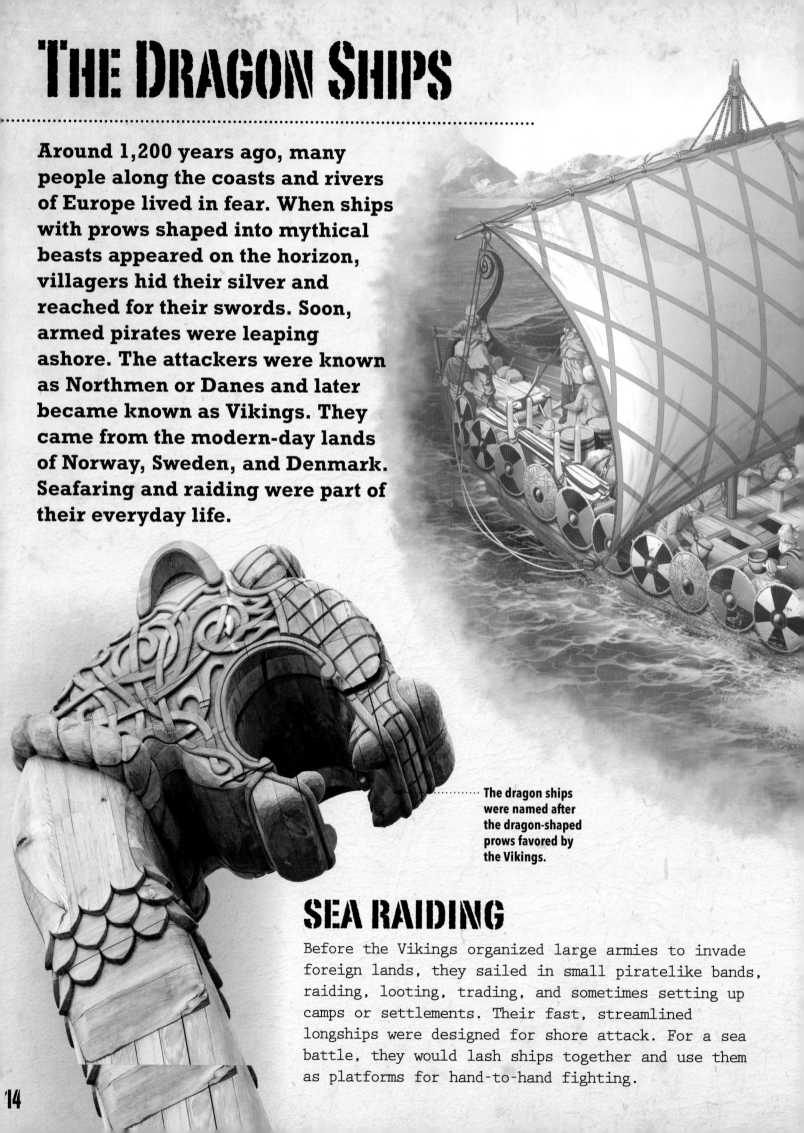

The dragon ships were named after the dragon-shaped prows favored by the Vikings.

SEA RAIDING

Before the Vikings organized large armies to invade foreign lands, they sailed in small piratelike bands, raiding, looting, trading, and sometimes setting up camps or settlements. Their fast, streamlined longships were designed for shore attack. For a sea battle, they would lash ships together and use them as platforms for hand-to-hand fighting.

A Viking ship steers through the icy waters of Scandinavia.

FIRST ATTACK

One of the earliest recorded Viking raids was the attack on the island of Lindisfarne in northeast England. The Vikings attacked the island's monastery in 793 CE.

The ruins of Lindisfarne Priory, which was attacked by the Vikings.

VIKING GODS

The early Vikings worshipped many gods. They had gods for thunderstorms, poetry, and even death. The Vikings often attacked undefended Christian monasteries, stealing gold and silver. Their victims may have been murdered or carried off as slaves.

VIKING TREASURE

Viking treasure hoards discovered today include gold and silver coins from all over Europe and the Middle East, jewelry, precious metals, and crosses from churches. Experts are still trying to figure out if they were fairly traded or stolen during violent raids and attacks.

A hoard of silver Viking jewelry and coins, discovered in Lancashire, England.

WHEN MIGHT WAS RIGHT

During the Middle Ages, Europe was often torn apart by wars. Wealthy families fought each other for thrones. Armies pillaged the land, and power was often won by brute force. Piracy was widespread, and it was often difficult to tell who was a pirate and who was supposed to be upholding the law.

TREASURE HUNTERS

Eustace the Monk (c. 1170–1217)

Eustace the Monk was from Boulogne, France. He was said to have studied black magic in Spain and to have made a pact with the devil. He later became a monk but was outlawed after a quarrel with Renaud de Dammartin, Count of Boulogne. He became a pirate in the English Channel and was hired by both English and French kings. In 1217, at the Battle of Sandwich, an English fleet attacked a convoy of French ships led by Eustace the Monk. He was caught and beheaded.

Eustace the Monk is caught and executed for piracy at the Battle of Sandwich in 1217.

THE LUNDY PIRATE

William de Marisco (Marsh) became a bitter enemy of King Henry III of England. In 1235, he fled to Lundy Island in the Bristol Channel, where he built a fort. He became a pirate, attacking ships in the Irish Sea. In 1242, he was captured, dragged through the streets of London from a horse, hanged, chopped into four pieces, and then burned.

Marisco Castle, which was built by the pirate William de Marisco, on Lundy Island.

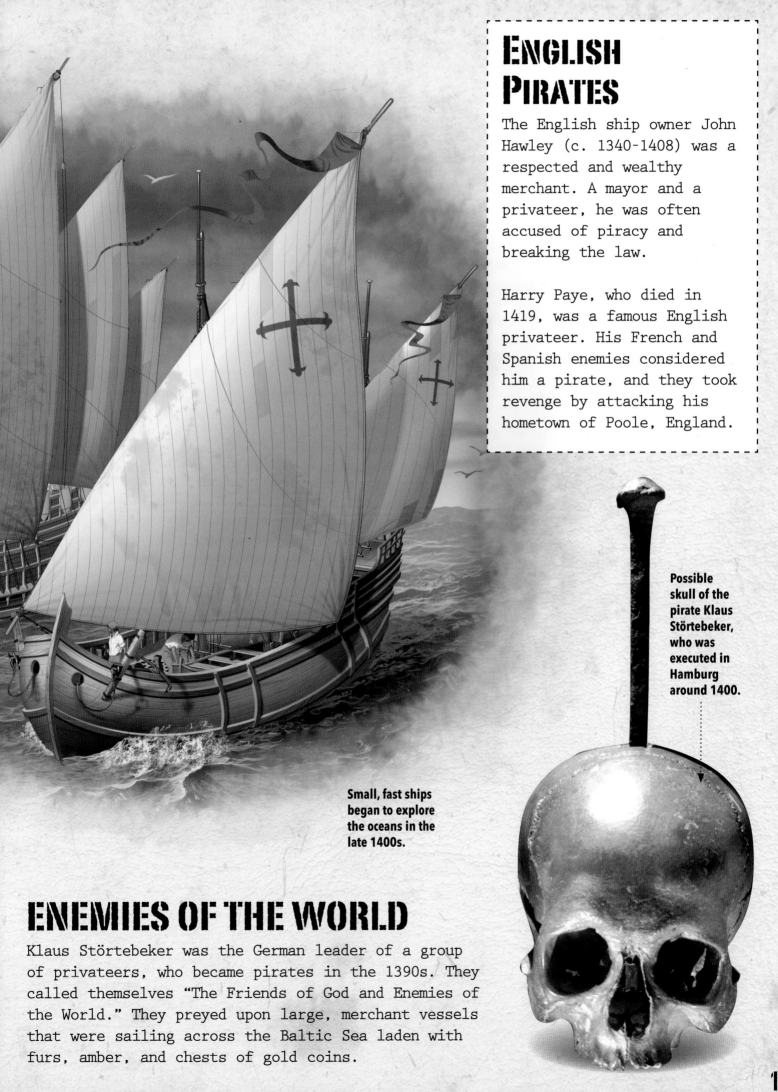

ENGLISH PIRATES

The English ship owner John Hawley (c. 1340-1408) was a respected and wealthy merchant. A mayor and a privateer, he was often accused of piracy and breaking the law.

Harry Paye, who died in 1419, was a famous English privateer. His French and Spanish enemies considered him a pirate, and they took revenge by attacking his hometown of Poole, England.

Possible skull of the pirate Klaus Störtebeker, who was executed in Hamburg around 1400.

Small, fast ships began to explore the oceans in the late 1400s.

ENEMIES OF THE WORLD

Klaus Störtebeker was the German leader of a group of privateers, who became pirates in the 1390s. They called themselves "The Friends of God and Enemies of the World." They preyed upon large, merchant vessels that were sailing across the Baltic Sea laden with furs, amber, and chests of gold coins.

BARBARY CORSAIRS

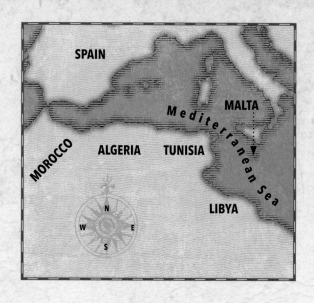

The Barbary or Berber Coast of North Africa stretched from Libya, Tunisia, and Algeria to Morocco. It was a center of piracy and privateering from the 1500s until the 1800s. The pirates and their ships were known as corsairs. They sailed fast galley ships powered by sails and oars, which were rowed by slaves.

WHO WERE THE CORSAIRS?

The corsairs were chiefly Berbers, Arabs, or Ottoman Turks. They were Muslims who attacked ships from the Christian countries of southern Europe and raided coastal settlements around the Mediterranean. They sailed as far north as the British Isles and Iceland. Captured prisoners were often enslaved or ransomed.

Pirates from North Africa close in on a galley ship belonging to Pope Julius II.

THE SALÉ ROVERS

The Dutch pirate Jans Janszoon (c. 1570-1641) was captured by Barbary corsairs in the Canary Islands. He joined the corsairs, became a Muslim, and called himself Murad Raïs. The corsairs based at the Moroccan port of Salé declared themselves an independent republic and elected Janszoon as Grand Admiral of the "Salé Rovers."

MALTESE CORSAIRS

The Mediterranean island of Malta was also a center of corsairs and raiders. However, they were Christians who attacked Muslims sailing along the Barbary Coast, and used their captives as slaves.

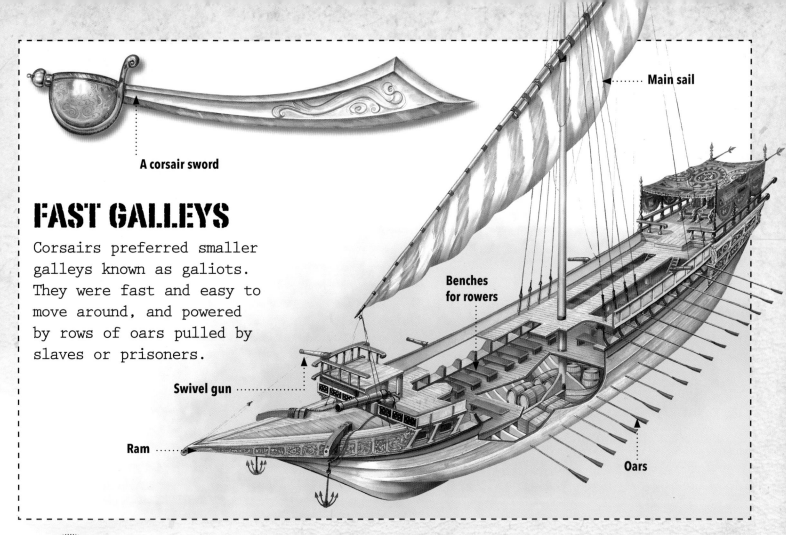

A corsair sword

FAST GALLEYS

Corsairs preferred smaller galleys known as galiots. They were fast and easy to move around, and powered by rows of oars pulled by slaves or prisoners.

Main sail

Benches for rowers

Swivel gun

Ram

Oars

TREASURE HUNTERS

The Barbarossa Brothers (Khizr c. 1478-1546, Aruj c. 1474-1518)

In 1504, two treasure galleys flying the flag of Pope Julius II were captured off the Italian island of Elba, and a Sicilian warship was captured off Lipari. These attacks were the work of two Barbary corsairs known to Europeans as the Barbarossa ("red-beard") brothers. They were half-Greek and half-Turkish, born on the island of Lesbos. Khizr, or Hayreddin, and Aruj, or Oruç, were coastal raiders and fierce attackers of shipping. They were at various times pirates, privateers, or naval officers. Khizr died fighting the Spanish, while Aruj became governor of Algiers and a respected admiral of the Ottoman Turkish fleet.

JOINING THE CORSAIRS
Over the years the Barbary corsairs were joined by pirates from northern Europe, including Englishmen John Ward (c. 1553–1622), Sir Francis Verney (1584–1615), and Dutchman Simon Danziker (c. 1579-1615).

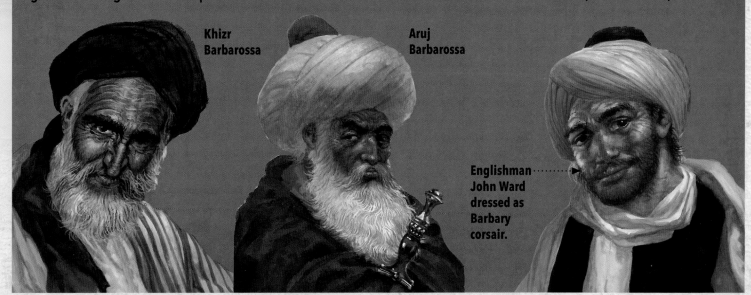

Khizr Barbarossa

Aruj Barbarossa

Englishman John Ward dressed as Barbary corsair.

SPANISH GALLEONS

In October 1492, the Italian explorer Christopher Columbus, sailing under the flag of Spain, landed in the Bahamas. This marked the start of the conquest of the Americas by Spanish, Portuguese, and other European invaders. Treasure was soon being shipped back to Europe. Spanish treasure ships were attacked by French and English privateers as well as pirates. The great age of piracy had begun.

Christopher Columbus, who is holding a cross, lands in the Bahamas.

A Spanish galleon

Main mast

Deck for cannon and guns

Bowsprit

Prow

Goods were stored on decks below the waterline.

CARGO CARRIERS

Spain's largest ships were called galleons. They had three or four masts and were armed with 60 cannons. Layers of decks enabled them to carry lots of cargo and a crew of around 200.

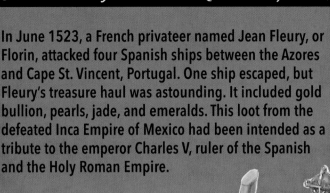
In June 1523, a French privateer named Jean Fleury, or Florin, attacked four Spanish ships between the Azores and Cape St. Vincent, Portugal. One ship escaped, but Fleury's treasure haul was astounding. It included gold bullion, pearls, jade, and emeralds. This loot from the defeated Inca Empire of Mexico had been intended as a tribute to the emperor Charles V, ruler of the Spanish and the Holy Roman Empire.

Spanish silver coins, known as Spanish dollars.

PIECES OF EIGHT

The silver mines of Potosí in Bolivia, opened by the Spanish in 1545, produced 60 percent of all the world's silver. The coins were minted by the Europeans in the Americas and remained in use in the 1600s and 1700s, and are forever associated with pirate treasure. They were known as Spanish dollars, or "pieces of eight," because they were worth eight Spanish "reales" (the Spanish currency).

Gold, silver, and jewels were stored in the treasure hold.

TREASURE HUNTERS
Sir Francis Drake (c. 1540–1596)

The English like to remember Sir Francis Drake as a privateer and a national hero. To the Spanish, whose ships he attacked, he was "El Draque" (the Dragon), a common pirate and a rogue.

TREASURE FLEETS
From 1566 to 1790, Spain's treasure ships traveled in heavily armed convoys numbering up to 100 vessels. Ships assembled off the coast of Cuba before crossing the Atlantic Ocean. Other treasure fleets sailed the Pacific Ocean, and it was in these waters in 1578 that Drake captured two Spanish ships laden with gold, silver, and jewelry.

BUCCANEERS OF TORTUGA

In the 1600s, many outlaws and desperadoes settled on islands in the Caribbean Sea. They included escaped slaves, criminals on the run, and sailors who had deserted their ships. They were rebels and adventurers, and some were very cruel and dangerous. They came from France, Portugal, Africa, Britain, and the Netherlands. The island of Tortuga became a notorious base for these "Brethren of the Coast." The rebels became known as boucaniers or buccaneers, named after the boucans or racks on which they smoked their meat.

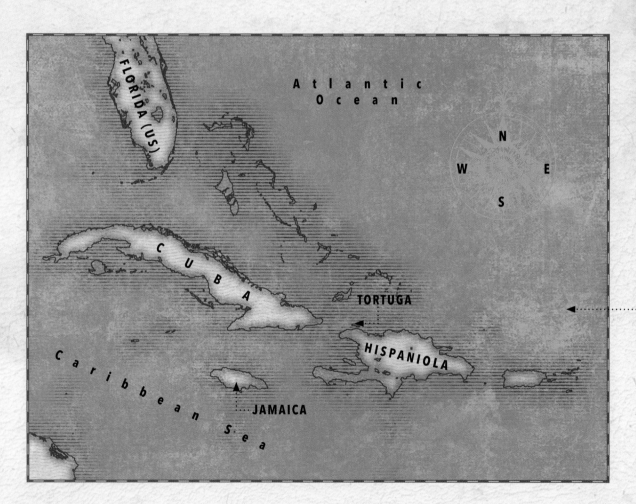

The Caribbean Islands where dangerous buccaneers preyed on passing ships.

THE ATTACKERS

The buccaneers soon turned their attention to the treasure-laden Spanish ships passing their shores. They built sailing canoes called piraguas, and from hidden coves they launched surprise attacks on the big, clumsy galleons. One of their tricks included jamming a rudder so that the ship was unable to steer.

A small pirate vessel, known as a sloop, attacks a much larger French merchant ship in the Caribbean Sea.

CRUEL AND DANGEROUS

The buccaneer Bartolomeo Português attacked Spanish ships in the 1660s. As a prisoner, he reportedly stabbed his Spanish guard in an attempt to escape.

Jean-David Nau (c. 1635-1668), also known as François l'Olonnois, was said to have cut out and eaten one of his victim's hearts.

The Dutch buccaneer Roche Brasiliano (c. 1630-1671), based in Jamaica, tortured his enemies with extreme cruelty, even roasting them alive.

Bartolomeo Português

Jean-David Nau

Roche Brasiliano

THE SPANISH MAIN

In 1655, the British captured Jamaica from the Spanish. They allowed the buccaneers to use Port Royal (near modern Kingston) as their base to keep up attacks on Spanish shipping.

Port Royal in Jamaica during the devastating earthquake of 1692.

THE PACIFIC PIRATE

In 1680, English buccaneers, including Bartholomew Sharpe, crossed Panama to the Pacific shore where they seized Spanish ships while sailing down the west coast of South America. Sharpe rounded the stormy waters of Cape Horn and sailed back to Barbados. At the time, Spain was not at war with England, so these were illegal acts of piracy. However, navigation charts that Sharpe had stolen from the Spanish were so valuable that he was pardoned of any crime.

CITY OF THE WICKED

Port Royal, Jamaica, was notorious for its brawling, gambling, and piracy. Much of the port was destroyed by an earthquake and tsunami in 1692. People believed the earthquake and tsunami were God's revenge.

TREASURE HUNTERS

Henry Morgan (c. 1635–1688)

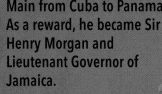

The ruthless Welsh privateer, Henry Morgan, was based in Jamaica and became famous at sea. He led buccaneer armies in devastating illegal attacks on Spanish ports along the Spanish Main from Cuba to Panama. As a reward, he became Sir Henry Morgan and Lieutenant Governor of Jamaica.

CREATOR OF A LEGEND

The story of the Spanish colonies known as the Spanish Main and their buccaneers was made famous by Alexandre Exquemelin (c. 1645–1707), a French or Dutch writer. He served with the privateer Henry Morgan and published a book about him in 1678.

The title page of *The History of the Bouccaneers of America* by Exquemelin.

FLAGS OF FEAR

The most famous period of piracy took place between the 1690s and the 1720s. At that time, many pirate captains began to fly their own personal flags from the mainmast. The flags were designed to strike terror in their victims, so many of them were based on tombstone carvings depicting skulls, bones, or skeletons. Some showed weapons such as daggers, spears, or cutlasses, the naval swords favored by pirates at that time. Others showed severed heads or bleeding hearts.

BLACKJACKS

Pirate flags were mostly black and were sometimes called blackjacks. Red, a symbol of blood and rebellion, was another traditional color. Since the Middle Ages, red flags at sea had signaled "no quarter," meaning no mercy would be shown in battle.

The menacing flag of a pirate ship shows a skull and crossed cutlass swords.

This cartoon from the 18th century has the pirate wearing the skull and crossbones so readers can easily identify him.

THE JOLLY ROGER

The skull-and-crossbones flag was sometimes called the Jolly Roger. Nobody is sure where this name came from. "Jolly Roger" was a nickname for any merry fellow, so it might refer sarcastically to a grinning skeleton. "Old Roger," like "Old Nick," was a nickname for the Devil. Some people think the name might have come from the French phrase "joli rouge," which means the "pretty red" flag.

The Jolly Roger, a flag used by many English pirate captains.

The flag used by the pirate John Rackham in the Caribbean.

Thomas Tew favored a flag showing an arm holding a short scimitar sword.

Bartholemew Robert's flag shows himself and death holding an hourglass.

The flag of Blackbeard depicts a skeleton piercing a heart while toasting the Devil.

A dagger, skull, and heart sit above a bone in this pirate flag.

FALSE FLAGS

To fool their enemies, pirates sometimes flew false national flags. At the last moment, just before the attack, they would raise the pirate flag, causing horror and panic.

TO THE SEVEN SEAS

The Caribbean Sea remained the center of piracy for many years. Its maze of islands and hidden inlets offered pirates safe havens. From here, they could ambush not only Spanish treasure ships but also merchant ships carrying precious cargoes from the new slave plantations and colonies set up by the French, British, and Dutch. Trade was now global, and so were the opportunities for piracy.

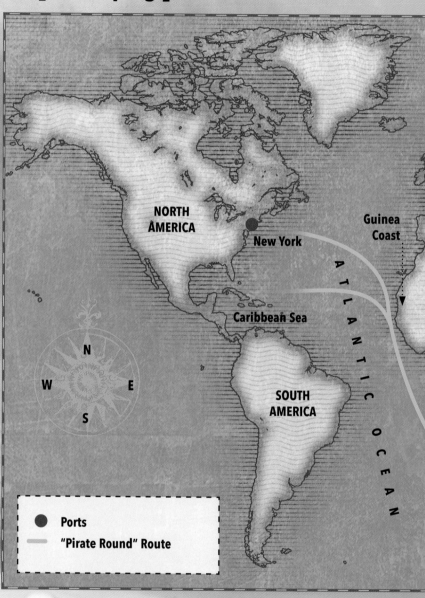

Ports

"Pirate Round" Route

WATCH YOUR BACK!

Thomas Anstis (d. 1723) left a trail of devastation from violent rampages around the Caribbean and North America. He escaped many battles with naval patrols, but in the end was murdered in his sleep by his own crew.

THE PIRATE ROUND

A regular sea route, known as the "Pirate Round," became established in the 1690s and 1700s. Pirate ships left the Caribbean or the Atlantic ports of North America. They sailed to West Africa and then south and east to Madagascar, the Indian Ocean, and the Red Sea, before returning home laden with stolen treasure.

A shipload of pirates raid a coastal settlement.

THE SECRET BACKERS

Why was it so hard to catch pirates? At the start of this period, naval forces were not large or organized enough to track down pirates around the world. Also, pirate voyages were sometimes secretly financed by powerful businessmen or corrupt colonial governors. They made sure that the pirates were never caught. In return, they would get a share of the profits.

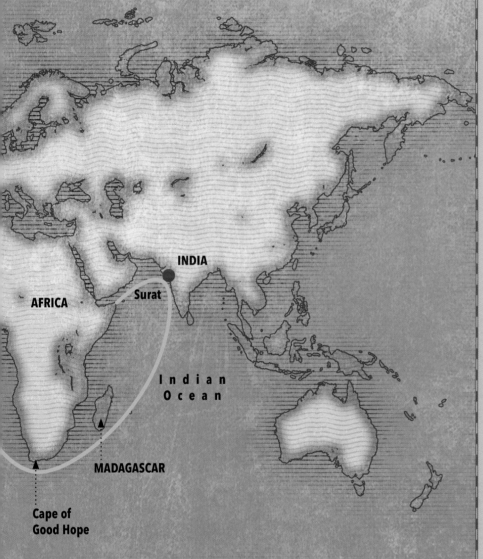

INDIA

AFRICA Surat

Indian Ocean

MADAGASCAR

Cape of Good Hope

The gentleman pirate Stede Bonnet

TREASURE HUNTERS

Stede Bonnet (c. 1688–1718)

Stede Bonnet was a "gentleman" pirate, a wealthy landowner from Barbados who spent the last two years of his life attacking ships in the Caribbean and North America. He was eventually hanged in Charleston in 1718.

THE STORMY NORTH ATLANTIC

In the early 1700s, the Atlantic coast of North America was made up of British colonies. These stretched from the Carolinas in the south to New England in the north. Pirates, often based in the Caribbean, Newfoundland, or the Bahamas, swarmed up and down the coast, attacking merchant ships and harbors. Many pirate cargoes were offloaded in Rhode Island, Long Island, or New York City.

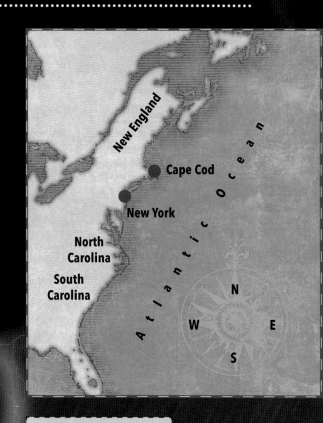

New England
Cape Cod
New York
North Carolina
South Carolina
Atlantic Ocean
N
W E
S

● Ports

TREASURE HUNTERS

Captain Samuel Bellamy (1689-1717)

Known as "Black Sam" because of his long, black hair, Samuel Bellamy was born in Devon, England. He settled in Cape Cod, Massachusetts. From there, he went treasure hunting off the Florida coast, and joined up with pirates in the Caribbean. He captured a slave ship, which had sold its human cargo and carried indigo, ivory, and four tons of gold and silver. Bellamy sailed the ship north, but it was wrecked off Cape Cod in a fierce storm, and 103 bodies were washed ashore.

CRUEL PIRATES
Other pirates in Atlantic waters included Bahamas-based Charles Vane, a cruel and stubborn man who was hanged in 1720.

Edward "Ned" Low of Boston (c. 1690-1724), known for torturing and killing his captives, was one of the most vicious pirate captains.

Charles Vane attacked ships in the Atlantic.

REBELS AND PRIVATEERS

By 1775, war had broken out between Great Britain and its American colonies. The colonists enlisted crews of privateers, whose ships were able to slip through the Royal Navy's blockade. The Commander in Chief of the U.S. Navy, Esek Hopkins, was also a former privateer. Britain was defeated by 1783.

Esek Hopkins, privateer and Commander in Chief of the U.S. Navy during the American Revolutionary War.

A tall sailing ship is caught in an Atlantic storm.

PIRATE FLEETS

Sometimes, pirates created small fleets with the ships they stole, but quarrels between pirate captains meant that alliances did not last very long. In other waters, particularly off the coast of China, pirate fleets could be much larger.

THE GULF OF GUINEA

In 1719, the Irish pirate known as Edward England captured ten ships between the Gambia River in West Africa and Cape Coast Castle (in what is now Ghana), before sailing on to the Indian Ocean. A new rash of piracy was breaking out along the West African coast.

Atlantic Ocean

Slave Forts

AFRICA

St. Louis

UPPER GUINEA

Sherbro

Whydah

Cape Coast

LOWER GUINEA

Gulf of Guinea

Benguela

N
W E
S

Edward England, who preyed on ships in the Gulf of Guinea.

SLAVE TRADE

At this time, the coast of the Gulf of Guinea was under the control of European companies, which built forts to control trade. The coast supplied slaves for the horrific trans-Atlantic trade. It also traded precious gold and ivory, and this soon attracted the marauding ships of the Pirate Round.

The fort of Cape Castle, built on the Gold Coast of West Africa, was a center for the Atlantic slave trade.

A British Royal Navy ship fires on the pirate ship of Bartholomew Roberts. He would lose his life in the battle.

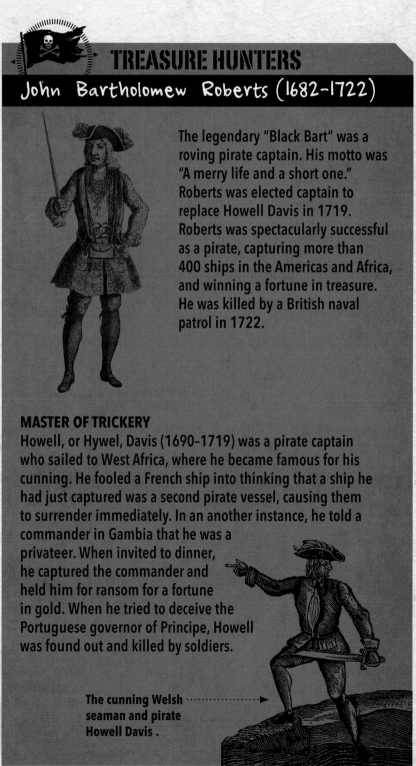

TREASURE HUNTERS
John Bartholomew Roberts (1682-1722)

The legendary "Black Bart" was a roving pirate captain. His motto was "A merry life and a short one." Roberts was elected captain to replace Howell Davis in 1719. Roberts was spectacularly successful as a pirate, capturing more than 400 ships in the Americas and Africa, and winning a fortune in treasure. He was killed by a British naval patrol in 1722.

MASTER OF TRICKERY
Howell, or Hywel, Davis (1690-1719) was a pirate captain who sailed to West Africa, where he became famous for his cunning. He fooled a French ship into thinking that a ship he had just captured was a second pirate vessel, causing them to surrender immediately. In an another instance, he told a commander in Gambia that he was a privateer. When invited to dinner, he captured the commander and held him for ransom for a fortune in gold. When he tried to deceive the Portuguese governor of Principe, Howell was found out and killed by soldiers.

The cunning Welsh seaman and pirate Howell Davis.

To India and Arabia

Many seafarers on the Pirate Round sailed on to the Indian Ocean. In India, pirates found valuable treasures including spices, silks, and luxuries of the Mughal Empire. Also sailing through these waters were the heavily armed merchant ships of the French, English, Portuguese, and Dutch. These were attacked by local ships along the Maratha coast of western India. Dismissed as pirates, the local ships were defending themselves against the greedy incomers.

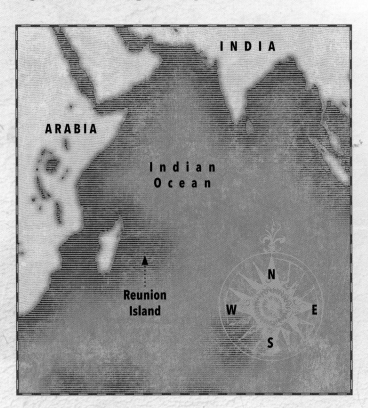

THE PRIZE

In 1720, the French pirate Olivier Levasseur joined English pirate John Taylor to capture a Portuguese galleon laden with treasure from Goa, India. The damaged ship, *Our Lady of the Cape*, had ditched its cannon in order to stop from sinking during a storm. It was being repaired on the island of Réunion, then known as Île Bourbon, in the Indian Ocean. This was one of the richest and easiest prizes in the history of piracy.

The ship's treasure also included a solid gold cross inlaid with diamonds and precious stones.

Captain Kidd steers his ship toward an Indian trading ship. Kidd has raised French flags to trick the larger galley.

TREASURE HUNTERS

Henry Avery, or Every (b. 1682) and Kanhoji Angri (c. 1669-1729)

Also known as "Long Ben" or "the Arch-Pirate," Henry Avery was an English pirate. In 1695, together with the pirate Thomas Tew, he attacked ships of India's Mughal Empire on their way to Arabia for the pilgrimage to Mecca. This was a brutal fight, in which many on both sides were killed. The captured treasure was probably worth more than $60 million in today's money. It is believed that Avery avoided capture but that he died in poverty.

KANHOJI ANGRIA
Maratha leader Kanhoji Angria (1669-1729) fought against the British, French, and Portuguese ships off the coast of India. As a result, he was labeled a pirate by his European enemies. He commanded hundreds of warships and remained undefeated despite many attempted attacks by European ships.

Kanhoji Angria, chief of the Maratha Navy in India.

PIRATE BASES

Pirates could not stop in any old port to repair their ships or pick up supplies. They needed to gather in remote places where they could share their loot and hide away from naval patrols. One famous pirate haven was at Nassau, on the island of New Providence in the Bahamas. In 1713, about 1,000 pirates were based there, making it the crime capital of the Americas.

A WORLD APART

Madagascar, a large island off the coast of Africa, was a chief haven on the Pirate Round.

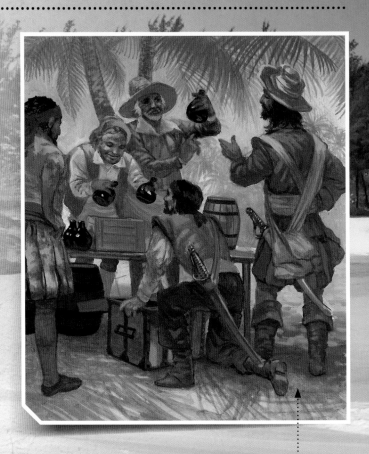

The notorious Scottish pirate Captain William Kidd trades stolen booty in Madagascar.

TREASURE HUNTERS

James Plantain

Plantain was an English pirate born in Jamaica. In 1715, he set up a base in Madagascar, north of St. Mary's Island. He called himself "King of Ranter Bay," but was forced to flee in 1728.

A PIRATE KINGDOM
Abraham Samuel, from the pirate ship *John and Rebecca*, landed in Madagascar in 1695. He was from Martinique in the Caribbean. He was of mixed African and European descent, but an elderly princess in Madagascar insisted he was her long-lost son and made him king. He engaged in piracy and in local wars until his death in 1705.

Madagascar, a tropical paradise where many pirates returned to live.

PIRATE PARADISE

During the early part of the 18th century, the island of Nassau was used as a base by pirates in the Caribbean. It became so strong that it declared itself a "Republic of Pirates" and was even goverened by its own code of conduct. The British took control and drove the pirates away in 1718.

Today, Nassau is a peaceful holiday destination that attracts cruise ships and thousands of tourists every year.

SAINT-MALO CORSAIRS

For hundreds of years, the fortified port of St. Malo in Brittany, France, was a base for French and Breton privateers. These corsairs sailed around the world attacking the enemies of France—often the English. The corsair René Duguay-Trouin (1673-1736) became a vice admiral in the French navy.

A nineteenth-century painting shows French corsairs marching with British prisoners and captured booty.

BLACKBEARD THE PIRATE (1680–1718)

Not many people have heard of Edward Teach. The notorious English pirate is much better known as Blackbeard, the rogue who spread terror around the Caribbean and the coasts of the American colonies. A big man with a thick, black beard, Teach was said to tie smoking fuses into his dreadlocks to terrify his victims.

NAVY PRIVATEER TO PIRATE

Teach was born in the busy port of Bristol in the west of England. He may have joined the Royal Navy in Jamaica in 1706 and probably served as a privateer during Queen Anne's War, which lasted until 1713. After that, Teach left Jamaica for the wild pirate haven of New Providence, in the Bahamas. In about 1716, he joined the pirate fleet of Benjamin Hornigold, commanding a sloop of six guns. The rogues were soon joined by another captain called Stede Bonnet and together they caused mayhem.

TO THE CAROLINAS

On November 28, 1717, Blackbeard captured a French slave ship from St Malo, *La Concorde*. He renamed it *Queen Anne's Revenge* and fitted it out with 40 cannons. In May 1718, Blackbeard's pirates blockaded the port of Charles Town (now Charleston) in South Carolina and demanded medical supplies be sent to him.

An eighteenth-century map of North and South Carolina. Legend has it that Blackbeard was killed on his sloop, near Ocracoke Inlet.

THE NET CLOSES

In 1718, Blackbeard negotiated a pardon from Governor Charles Eden of North Carolina, but he was soon back to his old piratical ways. Rumors spread that pirates were gathering off Ocracoke Island. Governor Alexander Spottiswood of Virginia asked the Navy to take action.

The ferocious battle between Blackbeard and First Lieutenant Robert Maynard.

Blackbeard's severed head hangs from the bowsprit of Maynard's ship.

A BATTLE TO THE DEATH

On November 22, 1718, First Lieutenant Robert Maynard cornered Blackbeard on board his sloop *Adventure*. In the fighting that followed, six of Maynard's men were killed and 10 wounded. Blackbeard fought furiously to the last. His head was severed and slung from the bowsprit of Maynard's sloop. Fourteen of the surviving 16 pirates were later rounded up and hanged.

WOMEN PIRATES

An old seafaring tradition declared that women should not go to sea, except as passengers. But throughout history, women have broken that rule. Some women organized piracy and even became pirates themselves.

The fearsome Marianne "Dieu-le-Veut" prepares for battle.

FEMALE WARRIORS

Anne or Marianne "Dieu-le-Veut" (meaning "God-Wills-It") lived from 1661 to 1710. She was a criminal from France, who was sent to Tortuga in the Caribbean Sea. There she married buccaneer Pierre Lelong, who was killed in a fight. In 1693, she married the Dutch pirate Laurens de Graaf, fighting fiercely beside him in hand-to-hand combat.

Kildavnet Castle, Achill Island, is one of a string of strongholds that Grace O'Malley is said to have built.

QUEEN OF CLARE ISLAND

Gráinne ní Mháille (c. 1530-1603) known in English as Grace O'Malley, was a fiery Irish noblewoman who owned a fleet of galleys. Her crews attacked passing ships from Clare Island and raided the Irish coast. When the English captured her sons and her half-brother, O'Malley sailed to London and met with Queen Elizabeth I at Greenwich Palace to negotiate peace, but she remained a rebel all her life.

CHINA'S DEADLY WIDOW

Zheng Yi Sao, "Madam Cheng," (1775-1844) grew up in China among the brutal pirate gangs that terrorized the Pearl River Delta and the South China Sea. Her husband built up a large fleet of wooden Chinese ships, known as junks. After his death in 1807, Madam Cheng was the ruthless ruler of one of the largest pirate alliances in history, with 300 armed junks and around 40,000 pirates.

British warships destroy Chinese junks in 1841.

The legendary female pirates, Anne Bonny (left) and Mary Read.

TREASURE HUNTERS

Anne Bonny (born c. 1700)
Mary Read (c. 1690-1721)

Anne Bonny was an Irish woman who moved with her father to Charleston, South Carolina. She married a pirate named James Bonny, but later ran off with a Bahamas buccaneer named Captain Rackham or "Calico Jack." In 1720, the couple met up with Mary Read. This English pirate, who, using the name Mark, pretended to be male, had served as a soldier in the Netherlands. The three of them stole a sloop and the women, dressed in male clothes, fought alongside the crew with axes, cutlasses, and pistols. Rackham was hanged in Jamaica in 1720. Bonny and Read escaped hanging because they were pregnant. Little is known of what happened to Anne Bonny, but Mary Read died of fever while in prison.

A Pirate Voyage

The crew members of most pirate ships were a wild bunch. They could include unwilling captives and victims of press gangs alongside mutineers, murderers, and rebels. Quarrels were common, and captains sometimes had fits of rage.

But crews were rewarded handsomely for their dangerous work. Pirates could often decide the rules of the ship and elect a new captain. They could have a share of plundered treasure and could sometimes receive compensation for injuries, such as the loss of a leg or an eye.

A crew member keeps a look out for enemy ships.

A seaman mends a rip in the ship's sail.

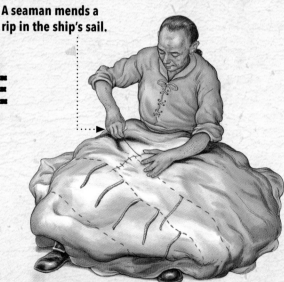

THE HARD LIFE

Life at sea in the 1700s meant long hours of hard and exhausting work, climbing the rigging, splicing frayed rope, scrubbing the deck, or keeping watch.

Sailors and pirates alike often slept in hammocks.

DOWN BELOW

Below deck it was dark and smelly, with rats, barrels, bales, and pools of water. Sailors slept where they could, on the deck or in hammocks. Hammocks were an invention of the Central American natives on the Spanish Main.

Pirates could not afford to be amateurs when it came to seafaring. Many were "old salts," with experience navigating across the world. Sometimes careless behavior occurred. In 1669, a spark exploded the gunpowder on Henry Morgan's flagship, the *Oxford*, blowing the ship sky-high and killing 200 crew members.

FRESH FOOD

The food might be scarce or didn't taste that great. But at island stops, barrels of fresh water could be taken on board, and stale biscuits could be replaced by fresh fish, fruit, or turtle soup. Chickens were kept on deck for their eggs.

Rats were a common sight on all ships in the 1700s.

SLOOPS AND CUTLASSES

Pirate ships were no different from the other vessels sailing the seas. The best pirate ships were speedy, easily maneuvered, and able to sail in shallows or creeks as well as the open sea. The single-masted sloops, built in Nassau or Jamaica in the 1700s, were ideal. For sea battles in open sea, larger ships with many cannons were useful.

Single mast

Captain's cabin

Cannon balls

Food and water stores

The crew prepare for the powerful blast of the cannon.

FIRING A CANNON

Heavy cannons were used to disable the enemy ship. An explosive charge was rammed down the barrel, followed by a cannonball. The charge was then lit, firing the cannon. The gun was mounted on a wheeled carriage and secured by a rope in order to withstand the powerful recoil.

BOARDING THE ENEMY

If pirates wanted to capture a ship or steal its treasure or crew, they did not want to blow it out of the water at the start of the battle. They would close upon it, throwing grappling irons into the rigging, and then swarm aboard. The fighting was hand to hand and savage.

Pirates board a ship and engage in a vicious battle with the crew on board.

Main sail

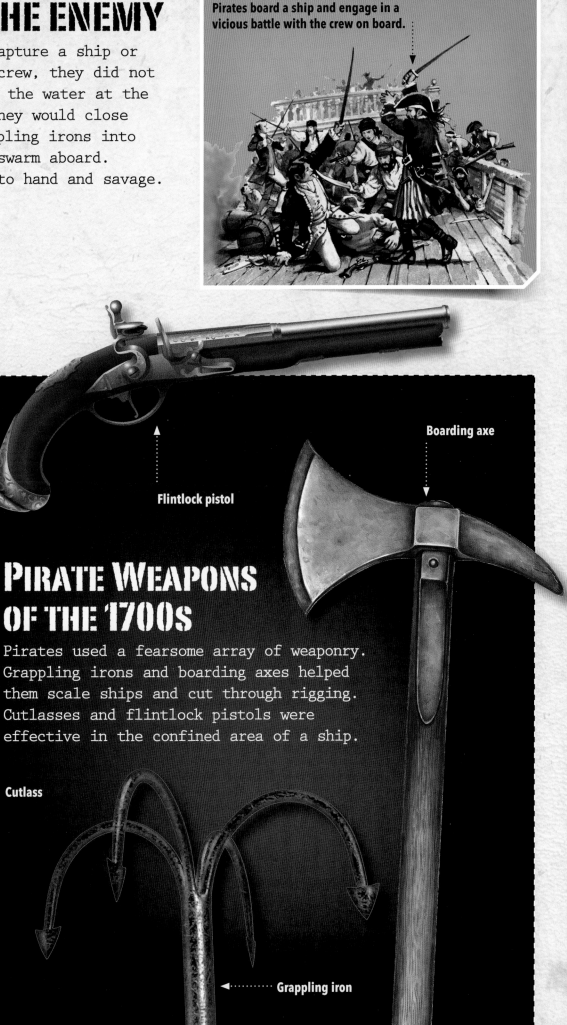

Flintlock pistol

Boarding axe

PIRATE WEAPONS OF THE 1700s

Pirates used a fearsome array of weaponry. Grappling irons and boarding axes helped them scale ships and cut through rigging. Cutlasses and flintlock pistols were effective in the confined area of a ship.

Cutlass

Grappling iron

PIRATE PUNISHMENTS

Pirates may seem to be romantic figures from history, but the reality was very different. They punished their own crews if they broke any rules, as well as their own captains if they did not supply any treasure. The pirates' victims might be treated well if they cooperated, but they were often humiliated, tortured, burnt, stabbed, or murdered.

If pirates recognized someone who had once treated them harshly, revenge could be especially violent. In 1718, Edward England and his crew came across Captain Skinner, who owed some of the crew payment for previous work. They pelted him with broken rum bottles before shooting him in the head.

Captain Henry Morgan captured and tortured residents of Porto Bello, Panama, in 1668.

WALKING THE PLANK

The best-known, but perhaps least common, punishment was called walking the plank. The victim's arms were bound so that he couldn't swim, or he was tied to a cannonball. He was then forced at sword point to walk a board above the waves, so that he fell to his death and drowned. This punishment is known to have been used by pirates on only two occasions.

The victim is thrown off the ship.

The victim is then dragged along the craggy keel.

KEELHAULING

Keelhauling was a punishment used by both naval officers and pirates. The victim was hauled by rope underwater and dragged against the ship's keel (the underside of the ship). This would lacerate his skin on the barnacles that encrusted the hull.

A man is abandoned on a deserted island.

Pirates force a captive to walk the plank, blindfolded and with arms bound.

MAROONED!

In the 1700s, a troublesome crew member might be abandoned on a deserted island with only the most basic supplies. He would have to fend for himself and hope that another ship would pass by and rescue him. This punishment was called marooning and was often fatal. A similar punishment was to cast people adrift in a small boat on the open ocean

Buried Treasure

In the 1700s, pirate treasure could include all sorts of goods such as tools, weapons, fancy clothes, textiles, charts, maps, even medicines, as well as shiny silver coins, gold bars, and jewels. The best treasure had to be easily divided among the pirates and readily disposed of without arousing suspicion. Precious metal objects could always be melted down.

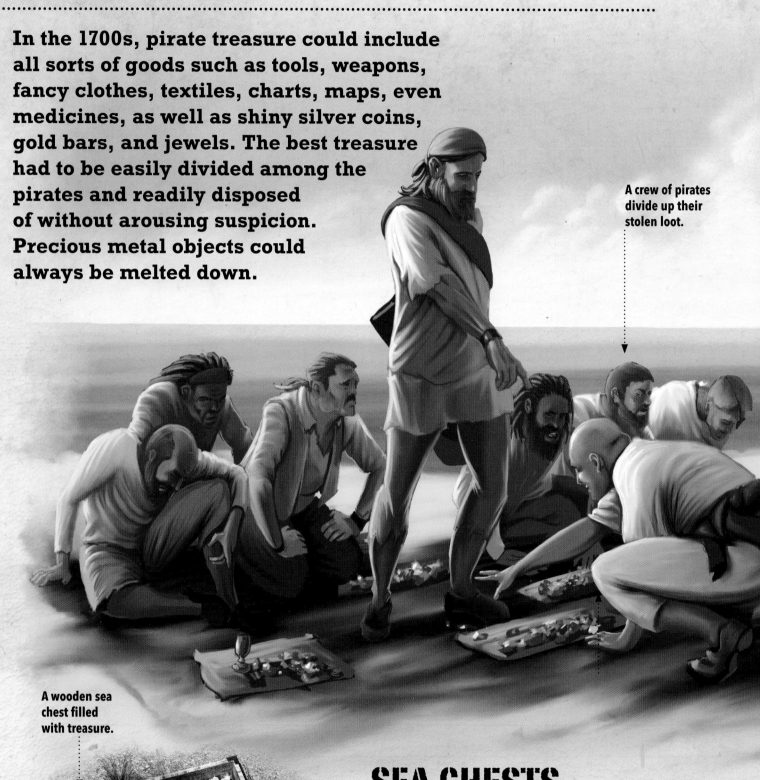

A crew of pirates divide up their stolen loot.

A wooden sea chest filled with treasure.

SEA CHESTS

In an emergency, some pirates may have buried their treasure on islands and remote beaches, intending to return at a later date. But old sea chests packed with hidden loot have never been uncovered, despite centuries of hunting for this notorious pirate treasure.

William Kidd was a Scottish sea captain who lived in New York City. In 1695, he was commissioned as a privateer to attack French merchant ships as well as to hunt pirates in the Indian Ocean. The voyage went horribly wrong. His rebellious crew urged him to turn into a pirate, and Kidd killed one of them, gunner William Moore, with a bucket. He was hanged as a pirate in London, in 1701.

THE TREASURE OF CAPTAIN KIDD

Few pirates have been linked with buried treasure as much as Captain William Kidd (1645-1701). For three centuries, treasure hunters have dug for his plunder. Experts believe Kidd buried some treasure on Gardiner's Island (off Long Island), New York. Since then, theories have spread like wildfire. Was the bulk of his treasure in Canada, on Grand Manan Island in the Bay of Fundy? Or was it buried on various islands in Connecticut? Did it exist at all? If it did, it is still out there waiting to be found.

Captain William Kidd

WHOSE TREASURE?

In 1927, a treasure hoard was found in the church of San José in Panama. Was it the English pirate Henry Morgan's treasure, stashed there during his attack on the city in 1671? It was most likely treasure hidden from Morgan and his buccaneers by panicking priests. Pirates, of course, used maps and charts, but no hand-scrawled treasure maps with the words "x marks the spot" have ever been discovered.

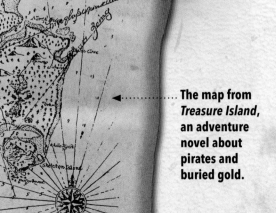

The map from *Treasure Island*, an adventure novel about pirates and buried gold.

Eastern Terrors

By the 1800s, the main remaining centers of piracy were in Asia. Many of these had existed for hundreds of years. The difference now was that European empire builders and traders were moving in, protected by the firepower of their warships. They tended to dismiss all their opponents as pirates, when it was more often a question of battles to control trade and win power.

EASTERN FLASHPOINTS

Eastern flashpoints included the Persian Gulf and the Straits of Hormuz, where British ships fought against fleets of large, armed wooden sailing vessels called dhows.

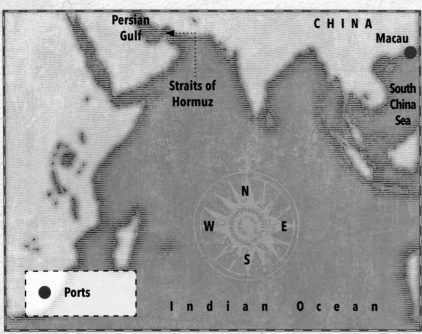

An pirate of Borneo in Southeast Asia.

Chinese pirates engage in a fierce sea battle in the 1800s.

Captured Chinese pirates await their fate at Kowloon, Hong Kong.

CHINESE PIRATES

Most true pirates in the 1800s were in the South China Sea around Macao and the Pearl River. They attacked all ships, raided coastal villages, and were noted for their cruel treatment of prisoners. Notorious Chinese pirates included Xu Yabao (or Chui Apoo, d. 1851) and Sha Wuzai (Shap'ng-Tsai, d. 1859).

Chui Apoo

FIGHTING JUNKS

The Chinese pirate ships were traditional junks, large wooden sailing ships, generally with three masts, a large rudder, and armed with many cannons. Pirate fleets also included hundreds of smaller boats, organized into squadrons, each with their own flag color.

A two-mast Chinese pirate boat

A large steering rudder is operated from the deck of the ship.

What Became of the Pirates?

There were few champions during the great age of piracy. Some buccaneers and sponsors of piracy became respected citizens. Few pirates escaped with their ill-gotten gains and lived long enough to enjoy them.

A pirate tombstone in Malacca, Malaysia.

A VIOLENT END

Many pirates gambled themselves back into poverty, drank themselves to death, or were swindled in turn by cleverer crooks. The majority of pirates were killed in fights, drowned at sea, died of illness, or were captured and hanged. Their piracy careers often lasted only two or three years.

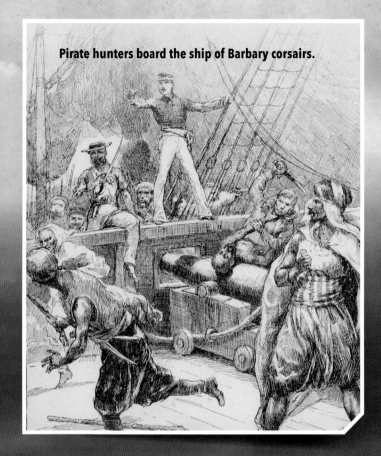

Pirate hunters board the ship of Barbary corsairs.

Peter Easton (c. 1570-1620)

Easton was an English privateer in the reign of Queen Elizabeth. In 1603, King James I came to the throne and canceled his privateering commission. Easton continued his work, even though this now made him a pirate. Based in Newfoundland, he ravaged shipping from Canada to the Caribbean, from the Mediterranean Sea to the Bristol Channel. He was in cahoots with the powerful Killigrew family of England. Easton ended up retiring in the south of France with so much gold that he bought himself the title of Marquis of Savoy.

PIRATE HUNTERS

Some pirates turned into pirate hunters. In 1718, the English privateer Woodes Rogers became governor of the Bahamas and removed the pirates from their base in New Providence. Naval patrols also became more and more successful at hunting down pirates.

THE FINAL BATTLES

The 1800s saw major sea battles, which aimed to put an end to piracy. The objective was to create a world ruled by the European powers and the United States of America. The reign of the Barbary corsairs at last came to an end with the repeated bombardment of Algiers. A British fleet destroyed Ras al Khaima in 1809. Another British fleet defeated the Chinese pirates off Tysami and at Pinghoi Creek in 1849.

GALLOWS AND GHOSTS

Sailors leaving the Port of London, England, in the 1700s saw grim reminders of the price to be paid for piracy. The tarred bodies of dead pirates were sometimes left hanging on the gallows by the riverside as a warning to others.

Trials of pirates were merciless. Often, many were publicly executed without a fair trial. Some died raging or weeping, but others put on an act for the crowd.

PIRATES IN COURT

Legal records of trials are the best way to track the true history of the pirates. The penalty for piracy varied through the ages, from crucifixion, torture, beheading, and hanging to drowning and dismemberment. Yet people were always so desperate for riches, and public officials were so corrupt, that men and occasionally women continued to risk everything by turning to piracy.

THE GHOST OF WILLIAM KIDD

The crimes of the pirates and their gruesome deaths have left behind many ghost stories and ghoulish legends. People claim to have seen the ghost of Captain Kidd near the former site of the old Execution Dock in Wapping, London, supposedly last used in 1830. Kidd's ghost has also been spotted across the Atlantic, at Gardiners Island, New York.

TALL TALES

At public executions, there were often people among the crowds selling broadsheets with lurid details of the pirate's adventures and downfall. These were a bit like the stories in the popular press of today, and ballads sung about pirates were the pop songs of the 1600s and 1700s.

An illustration from Captain Johnson's popular book about pirates.

CRIME STORIES

In 1724, *A General History of the Robberies and Murders of the Most Notorious Pyrates* was published by Captain Charles Johnson. People were thrilled and shocked by these accounts, and the book is still in print today.

The fictional Captain Hook was the pirate captain in J. M. Barrie's *Peter Pan*.

THE PERFECT VILLAIN

In J.M. Barrie's *Peter Pan* (1904), the character of Captain Hook is a comic pirate who has become loved by generations of children, whether on stage or screen. Barrie knew children were fascinated by pirates, and he gave the character a hook to replace the hand that was eaten by a crocodile.

TREASURE ISLAND

In 1881, the Scottish author Robert Louis Stevenson wrote an exciting story called *Treasure Island*. Ever since, this book has shaped our idea of what pirates were like with eye patches, wooden legs, pet parrots, and treasure maps.

Treasure Island features one of fiction's most famous pirates, Long John Silver.

The cover of Stevenson's classic adventure story about pirates.

GALLANT PIRATES

The first pirate humor appeared in the 1880s in an opera by Gilbert and Sullivan called *The Pirates of Penzance*. It is a funny tale of a tenderhearted band of pirates from Cornwall, England and their young apprentice Frederic.

The Gilbert and Sullivan opera *The Pirates of Penzance* is still performed across the world.

SHIPWRECK EVIDENCE

Just as the fantasy version of piracy was beginning to lead us far from the truth, a series of amazing discoveries by marine archaeologists and treasure hunters has led us back to historical reality.

BOY PIRATE

In 1983, Sam Bellamy's *Whydah Galley* was discovered off Cape Cod, where it had sunk in a storm in 1718. Divers recovered the ship's bell, weapons, private possessions, and the remains of a boy believed to be 11-year-old John King, the youngest known pirate. Reports in 2016 suggested that more treasure had been located, but this has yet to be proven.

The discovery of *Whydah Galley*'s bell confirmed the findings were a pirate shipwreck.

The pirate ship *Whydah Galley* is caught up and eventually sunk in an Atlantic storm.

KIDD'S GALLEY?

In 1698, Captain Kidd's *Adventure Galley* was deliberately sunk, or scuttled, off the coast of Madagascar. A possible wreck was investigated between 1999 and 2015, but its identity as Kidd's ship has yet to be confirmed.

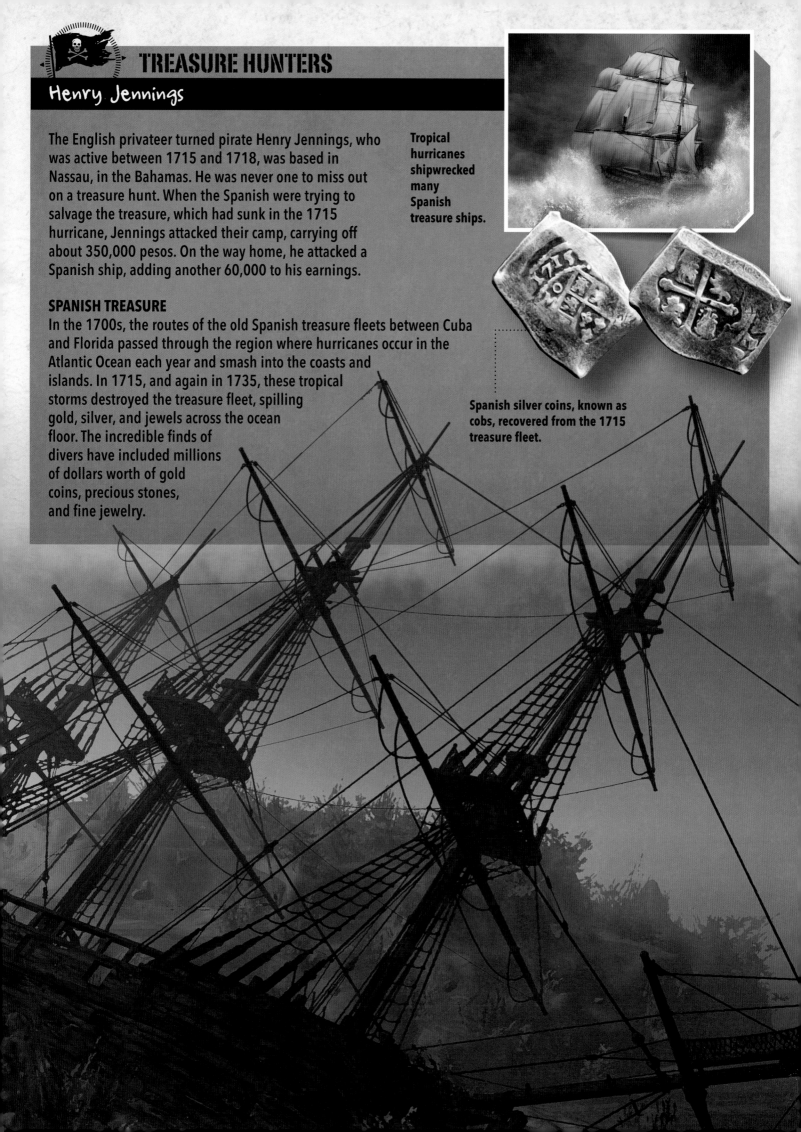

TREASURE HUNTERS

Henry Jennings

The English privateer turned pirate Henry Jennings, who was active between 1715 and 1718, was based in Nassau, in the Bahamas. He was never one to miss out on a treasure hunt. When the Spanish were trying to salvage the treasure, which had sunk in the 1715 hurricane, Jennings attacked their camp, carrying off about 350,000 pesos. On the way home, he attacked a Spanish ship, adding another 60,000 to his earnings.

Tropical hurricanes shipwrecked many Spanish treasure ships.

SPANISH TREASURE

In the 1700s, the routes of the old Spanish treasure fleets between Cuba and Florida passed through the region where hurricanes occur in the Atlantic Ocean each year and smash into the coasts and islands. In 1715, and again in 1735, these tropical storms destroyed the treasure fleet, spilling gold, silver, and jewels across the ocean floor. The incredible finds of divers have included millions of dollars worth of gold coins, precious stones, and fine jewelry.

Spanish silver coins, known as cobs, recovered from the 1715 treasure fleet.

PIRACY TODAY

Piracy hasn't disappeared completely. Since the 1990s, it has increased yet again. The reasons include poverty, a breakdown in international law and order, the fallout from wars and terrorism, and the loss of local fishing grounds to international trawling.

British armed forces approach a large vessel suspected of being operated by pirates in the Indian Ocean.

Cargo ships in the Indian Ocean have been targeted by pirates.

DANGEROUS WATERS

Governments and authorities around the world have stepped up their activities in the fight against piracy. Once-dangerous waters are patrolled by multinational forces and many large cargo ships have armed security forces on board.

SOMALI PIRACY

In the Indian Ocean, shipping has been targeted by pirates from Somalia in East Africa. At first, small valuable items were stolen, but later whole ships and cargoes were ransomed for billions of dollars. Individuals were captured too, sometimes in coastal raids, and held hostage until a ransom was paid. Piracy has now spread to West Africa and the Gulf of Guinea.

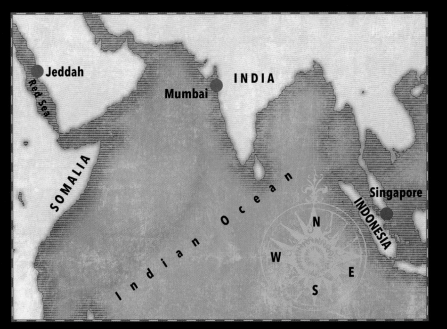

Area of Somalian pirate attacks.

● Ports
░ Area of pirate activity

In 2008, the *MV Faina* was captured by Somali pirates. The hijacked crew were rescued by the U.S. Navy.

THE REALITY

In Southeast Asia and the Caribbean, luxury yachts have been attacked and robbed, with passengers sometimes murdered.
The modern rise in piracy is a timely reminder that although we all enjoy stories of ancient piracy, the reality was always ugly and brutal, just as it is today.

MADAGASCAR PIRATE HAVEN

SETTLED BY: James Plantain and other pirates

WHEN: 1715

WHERE: Madagascar

MAP GRID REFERENCE: H, 5

1715 SPANISH TREASURE FLEET

ATTACKED BY: Henry Jennings

WHEN: July 1715
WHERE: Atlantic Oceans

MAP GRID REFERENCE: C, 5

PIRATE FLAG

FLOWN BY: Blackbeard

WHEN: 1713-1718

WHERE: Caribbean and Americas

MAP GRID REFERENCE: A, 6